Of all the towns and villages in Derbyshire, A jewel in the crown. It excels in its distingu literary associations and its matchless setting. Its church is almost of the dimensions of a cathedral and contains one of the finest series of monumental effigies in England, and Queen Elizabeth's Grammar School (now a comprehensive) was founded in 1583 and its original premises (still part of the school) is one of the distinguished buildings in Church Street. Ashbourne retains probably the only relic of original football in the strange game which has been played from time immemorial around the town and in its immediate surroundings.

THE TOWN OF ASHBOURNE

Ashbourne has had many distinguished visitors over the centuries including King Charles I, his descendant Prince Charles Edward Stuart, Dr. Johnson, James Boswell, Izaak Walton and Mrs. Gaskell to name but a few. Today the town is visited each year by many thousands who come to enjoy its weekly markets, to visit some of its fine shops and in general to enjoy the ambience of an unspoilt country town.

The frequent visits of Dr. Johnson to Ashbourne are not the only literary associations which the town can claim. It is thinly disguised as 'Oakbourne' in George Eliot's *Adam Bede* and Thomas Moore, to whom Lord Byron addressed the question quoted on page 16, was supposed to have been so impressed with the bells of Ashbourne Church that they inspired his song *Those Evening Bells*.

The town of 'Essenburne' is mentioned in Domesday Book along with its church and priest and subsequently was always a place of some importance being a centre for trade and social intercourse for a wide surrounding area, the nearest place of any consequence being Bakewell, 19 miles due north, Wirksworth 13 miles north east and Derby, 13 miles south east.

The Mansion's former owner Dr. John Taylor

The Mansion with (inset) James Boswell and Dr. Samuel Johnson (lower right)

A lyrical view of Ashbourne Hall in the early 1800s

These were considerable distances in pre-motor days. In the 17th century Ashbourne's population exceeded that of Derby for a time. Today agriculture and a certain amount of light industry make up the life-blood of the town, to which must be added tourism.

The great parish church does not form the fulcrum of the town as do some churches. It stands a little off-centre, but its spire nevertheless adorns certain views of the town particularly the main shopping area, St. John's Street. Whichever way you look at this street, it is an architectural feast with the now rare type of inn-sign of the 'Green Man and Black's Head' straddling the road. Looking westwards, the soaring church spire makes an interesting eyecatcher in the distance and the buildings to be seen are practically all 18th or early 19th century. Further down towards the church, St. John's Street turns into Church Street and we enter the oldest part of Ashbourne with the original Grammar School building, almshouses and some distinguished 18th century town houses of prosperous merchants and the local gentry. The church itself stands, somewhat aloof, at the perimeter of all this.

Prince Charles Edward Stuart, a visitor to Ashbourne Hall in 1745

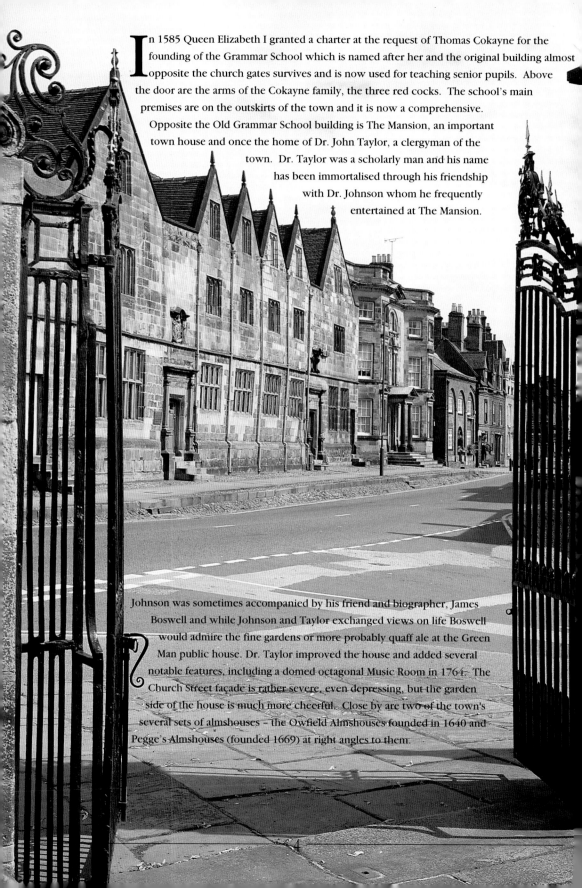

In 1585 Queen Elizabeth I granted a charter at the request of Thomas Cokayne for the founding of the Grammar School which is named after her and the original building almost opposite the church gates survives and is now used for teaching senior pupils. Above the door are the arms of the Cokayne family, the three red cocks. The school's main premises are on the outskirts of the town and it is now a comprehensive.

Opposite the Old Grammar School building is The Mansion, an important town house and once the home of Dr. John Taylor, a clergyman of the town. Dr. Taylor was a scholarly man and his name has been immortalised through his friendship with Dr. Johnson whom he frequently entertained at The Mansion.

Johnson was sometimes accompanied by his friend and biographer, James Boswell and while Johnson and Taylor exchanged views on life Boswell would admire the fine gardens or more probably quaff ale at the Green Man public house. Dr. Taylor improved the house and added several notable features, including a domed octagonal Music Room in 1764. The Church Street façade is rather severe, even depressing, but the garden side of the house is much more cheerful. Close by are two of the town's several sets of almshouses – the Owfield Almshouses founded in 1640 and Pegge's Almshouses (founded 1669) at right angles to them.

Detail of Elizabeth I's Charter to the Grammar School

Nearer the centre, nos. 16-22 Church Street are the Clergymen's Widows Almshouses, built in the 1750s.

As Church Street turns into St. John's Street, a left-hand entry into the Market Place is called Victoria Square formerly The Shambles or the Butchery (there are still meat purveyors there) – a pleasing jumble of alleys and buildings. Looking back into St. John's Street, a good view can be had of the Green Man and Black's Head, a mid-Georgian building which would have been new when Boswell visited it and pronounced it 'a very good inn'.

Beyond the turning into Victoria Square, Buxton Road turns off sharply north and forms one side of the wide and handsome Market Place. Here again most of the buildings are Georgian or early 19th century with the exception of the ornate Victorian town hall and the George and Dragon with its dramatic carved sign.

Ashbourne was never under the paternal eye of some great noble landowner, it being just outside the orbits of the Earls of Shrewsbury, the Dukes of Devonshire and the Dukes of Rutland, but nevertheless there were a number of less important families living near who exerted their influence in various ways and left us their houses.

The Cokaynes long since abandoned the town and only their splendid monuments are left in the church

Carved sign to the George & Dragon

to remind us of their importance, and their three heraldic cocks appear now and again on buildings in the town. The family's only connection with the town is now in the title of the head of the family – Lord Cullen of Ashbourne.

The Cokaynes' successors, the Boothbys, lived at their old home Ashbourne Hall until 1846 when the 9th Baronet, Sir William Boothby, died. A hundred years before, Prince Charles Edward Stuart stayed at the Hall before entering Derby on his ill–fated attempt on London. Ashbourne Hall survives only in a fragment and its park and lake are now public property, being the town's own park with a sports pavilion and lake. It was purchased as a memorial for those who fell in the Great War and the actual War Memorial Stands close to the road.

One of Ashbourne's most historic secular buildings is now known as The Ashbourne Gingerbread Shop, one of the places where the famous Ashbourne gingerbread is on sale. It is a timber-framed structure of considerable antiquity.

It is the distinguished calibre of the shops in the town which attracts shoppers and visitors from far afield to buy smart and fashionable clothes for either sex or to buy the best quality fishing tackle and gear or to sample the splendid range of cheeses on sale.

The Gallery is a fairly new development of small shops and boutiques in quaint old cobbled narrow alleys.

Ashbourne is also renowned for its antique shops, with one specialising in old prints.

The renowned Gingerbread shop, one of the town's oldest buildings

Bisecting the town is a little tributary of the Dove called the Henmore Brook. Once Ashbourne was to the north of the Brook and over the water was a hamlet called Compton. Now much of the river is underground to avoid flooding and though the name Compton is retained, the small separate village is now inextricably part of the town. Compton is approached via Dig Street (where will be found, in Workhouse Yard, Cary's Wine Bar and Bistro named after John Cary the famous local cartographer) over Compton Bridge with an attractive view of Henmore Brook.

Bandstand in the Memorial Park.

Wine Bar on Henmore Brook

*Pegge's Almshouse,
founded in 1669*

*The Vines, a Georgian
house in Church Street*

Ashbourne was granted a charter allowing markets on Thursdays and Saturdays and on certain other days of the year, in 1257. Here, in the Market Place, will be found the offices of the local Tourist Board where help and advice may be had.

When John Wesley visited the town he is said to have preached a sermon in the Market Place.

*The Market
Place on
Market day*

*The old and
the new in
Dig Street*

To cater for all the people who visit Ashbourne for its shopping and its many other attractions, the town is well served with hotels and restaurants. A shopping and office complex will be found off Dig Street (a corruption of Ditch Street) called Shaw Croft and off Shaw Croft Car Park is Derwent Crystal Ltd., where visitors may watch the intricate art of glass-blowing in action. On the other side of the road is a fine example of an 18th century house in Compton, now occupied by Lloyds Bank.

Situated further out on the Clifton Road are the bore holes, from which the renowned Ashbourne Mineral Water is pumped to the surface. This increasingly fashionably drink, either still or sparkling, is now as well known as Malvern Water.

A t 212 ft, the spire of St Oswald's is exactly the height of Repton – what a dramatic landmark it would have made if the church had been sited on one of the hills beneath which Ashbourne nestles.

Within is a most curious juxtaposition of architecture. Almost like a living sketch from an archaeologist's notebook, the styles of various periods jostle with one another to form a curious whole.

Approaching up the aisle it is difficult to know where to look first. Ahead, through the tower arches, is what is obviously a beautiful chancel, the colour of the east window against the grey stone contrasting as richly as a clump of poppies in a cornfield. To the left, through lovely arches and a decorated wood screen, an exciting glimpse of the recumbent figures of the many memorials in the Boothby Chapel. To the right, opening up through yet more arches, the vision of flowing stone tracery in a great south window, all the more impressive for being filled with plain glass. On either hand, as you approach, are the massive piers of the great square tower, and passing into the crossing, a

vista to both right and left of wide arcaded transepts. Turning around to face the west, the most striking feature is the distinct sheering away of the building line of the nave towards the north, although this does, at least, have the effect of emphasising the fine arcading of the south aisle dwindling in interesting perspective in the direction of the west door. Descending the shallow steps from the altar we have again the fascinating

OSWALD

'We went to the church at Ashbourne, which is the largest and most luminous that I have seen in any town of the same size' – Sunday September 21st 1777.

James Boswell

interplay of arches as we approach the crossing and see through the choir the Boothby Chapel and north transept.

The Boothby Chapel is entered through the screen which divides it from the north transept proper. In the east wall are two lovely triple lancet windows with detached shafts and matching moulding, through which the morning sun slants onto the assembled monuments.

The font

Earliest of these monuments is one to John and Edmund Cokayne, with the interesting costume of its two recumbent alabaster figures. The Cokayne family lived in Ashbourne from the middle of the twelfth to the end of the seventeenth century when Sir Aston Cokayne, in financial difficulties from his fervent support of the Royalist cause, sold his Ashbourne estates. Sir John Cokayne, represented on this altar tomb in fourteenth century costume, was MP for Derbyshire for many years, while his son, Edmund, who appears in a pointed basinet and tippet of mail, was killed at the Battle of Shrewsbury in 1403. Next to his tomb is that of Edmund's son Sir John Cokayne, who died in 1447 and his wife Jane.

An altar tomb of Purbeck marble is the memorial to Sir Thomas and Dame Barbara Cokayne. Sir Thomas, whose fame is inscribed both on the tomb and in similar rhyming extravagances on a brass plate on the wall, was knighted on the field of battle by Henry VIII at Tournay and played his colourful part at the Field of the Cloth of Gold. His eldest son, Francis with his wife Dorothy, are represented in another altar tomb which displays fine brass effigies of the pair with their six children. The latest of the Cokayne memorials is one of Renaissance design on the north wall of the transept. This is to Sir Thomas, one of the founders of Queen Elizabeth's Grammar School, and his wife Dorothy, daughter of Sir Humphrey Ferrers of Tamworth who are depicted facing one another in a kneeling posture with their three sons and seven daughters kneeling below them.

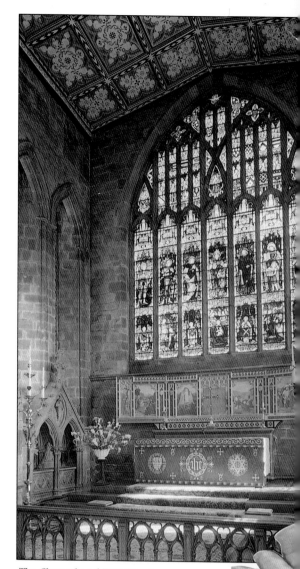

The Chancel and East Window

The Arms of the Cokayne family (situated above the old Grammar School door)

The Boothby family, who bought Ashbourne Hall from the Cokaynes, have a number of memorials in this chapel, but, with one exception, none of any great interest. The exception is, of course, the nationally-famous marble sculpture to Penelope, which draws more visitors to St Oswald's than any other feature. In pure white Carrara marble, the work of Thomas Banks, RA, this child figure, cheek on pillow, tiny feet peeping from beneath the flowing folds of her frock, probably evokes more sentimental compassion than any memorial in the country.

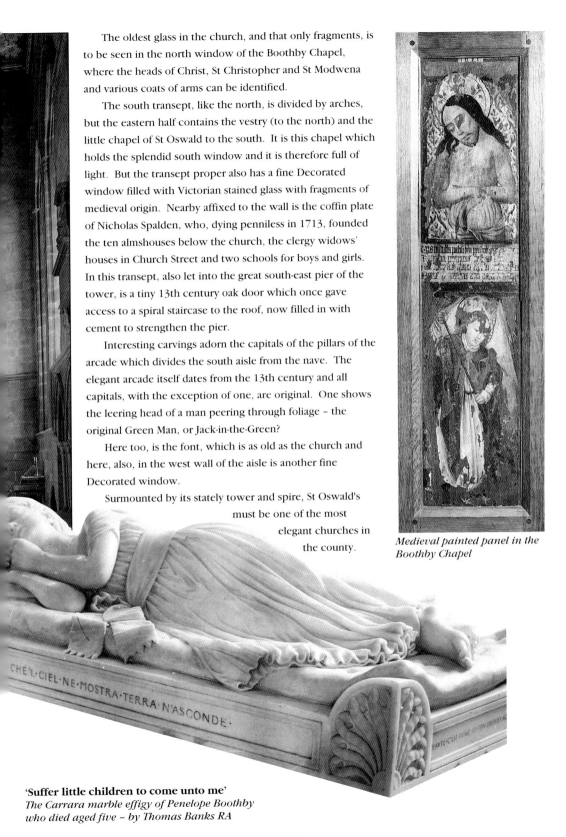

The oldest glass in the church, and that only fragments, is to be seen in the north window of the Boothby Chapel, where the heads of Christ, St Christopher and St Modwena and various coats of arms can be identified.

The south transept, like the north, is divided by arches, but the eastern half contains the vestry (to the north) and the little chapel of St Oswald to the south. It is this chapel which holds the splendid south window and it is therefore full of light. But the transept proper also has a fine Decorated window filled with Victorian stained glass with fragments of medieval origin. Nearby affixed to the wall is the coffin plate of Nicholas Spalden, who, dying penniless in 1713, founded the ten almshouses below the church, the clergy widows' houses in Church Street and two schools for boys and girls. In this transept, also let into the great south-east pier of the tower, is a tiny 13th century oak door which once gave access to a spiral staircase to the roof, now filled in with cement to strengthen the pier.

Interesting carvings adorn the capitals of the pillars of the arcade which divides the south aisle from the nave. The elegant arcade itself dates from the 13th century and all capitals, with the exception of one, are original. One shows the leering head of a man peering through foliage – the original Green Man, or Jack-in-the-Green?

Here too, is the font, which is as old as the church and here, also, in the west wall of the aisle is another fine Decorated window.

Surmounted by its stately tower and spire, St Oswald's must be one of the most elegant churches in the county.

Medieval painted panel in the Boothby Chapel

'Suffer little children to come unto me'
*The Carrara marble effigy of Penelope Boothby
who died aged five – by Thomas Banks RA*

CHE·L·CIEL·NE·MOSTRA·TERRA·N'ASCONDE·

FISHING IN THE DOVE AND ITS TRIBUTARIES

Izaak Walton

Izaak Walton immortalised the Dove and made it a place sacred to fishermen – *sacrum piscatoribus*. Walton was born in 1593 and his famous work 'The Compleat Angler' first appeared in 1653. Walton, the former ironmonger's apprentice, became friends with Charles Cotton, a Staffordshire gentleman some 30 years his junior. Cotton was an amateur poet and writer and wrote burlesques of Virgil and pieces on Derbyshire. He wrote an imaginary conversation between a passer-by and a fisherman (*Viator and Piscator*) in 1676 and this was incorporated into the 5th edition of Walton's book.

Charles Cotton

*'My river still through the same channel glides
Clear from the tumult, salt and dirt of tides'*
Charles Cotton

All the places associated with Walton and all the best fishing are within easy distance of Ashbourne but access to the fishing is strictly limited. Guests staying at the Izaak Walton Hotel near Ilam or at the Charles Cotton Hotel at Hartington may obtain permission to fish the waters, otherwise one has to become a member of one or other of the angling clubs. This is not easy as there is frequently a waiting list.

The Ashbourne Fly-fishers' Club has fishing rights on the Henmore and Bentley brooks, both tributaries of the Dove, and there are other clubs. No day tickets are available. These restrictions are only common sense. If everybody were allowed free access to the fishing in these waters, there would very soon be nothing left to fish.

The Council has leased the fishing rights of the lake in the town's recreation ground to the Ashbourne Wine Tavern Angling Club for coarse fishing.

Walton died in his ninetieth year in 1683 and his famous treatise on the art of fishing is still read.

The Compleat Angler or the Contemplative man's Recreation.

ROYAL SHROVETIDE FOOTBALL

Commemorativ[e] postcard of the Prince of Wales' visit in 1928

The inhabitants of Ashbourne made their own amusements before the railway came and pretty crude some of them were. Bull-baiting and prize-fighting were popular but the former was made illegal in 1835 and ended though prize-fighting went on after local bylaws were enacted to prevent it. Being so close to Staffordshire the miscreants could hop over the border and escape prosecution. In the fullness of time this barbarous sport, too, disappeared but Ashbourne's own brand of very rough, tough football has survived.

It is held annually each Shrovetide and is thought to be a survival of medieval street football which took place between rival villages and often ended in bloodshed, though other authorities suggest a much earlier origin with ritualistic and tribal overtones, the ball originally being a human head!

In the 19th century there were at least 36 public houses in the town and several beer houses so it is not surprising to learn that Victorian Shrovetide Football invariably caused a great deal of disruption in the town and was the occasion of much drunken brawling and damage to property. Several attempts to ban the game were foiled, notably in 1860, so that today it still goes on though without quite so much savagery.

The 'Uppards' and 'Down'rds' fight it out!

An ancient specimen of a Shrovetide football

*'The police appeared perfectly intimidated by the crowd – and would have been
had there been 50 of them'.* – Derby Mercury of Feb. 22 1860.

There are few rules and in former times the only rule was that you did not kill
your opponent! The ball is specially made to withstand the poundings and is made
of leather crammed tightly with cork shavings. To start the game the ball is 'turned
up', i.e. thrown into the crowd, usually by some celebrity. H.R.H. the
Prince of Wales turned up the ball in 1928 since when the game has adopted the pre-
fix 'Royal'.

The teams consist of those who live north of the Henmore Brook – the 'Uppards',
and those who dwell south of it – the 'Down'rds'. The respective goals are at
Sturton Mill and Clifton Mill, being three miles apart.

The celebrity is traditionally given luncheon at *The Green Man
and Black's Head* pub when the special Shrovetide song is sung
and then a large crowd assembles at Shaw Croft to see him turn
up the ball after a rendering of the National Anthem. Then all Hell
is let loose and inevitably most contenders end up in the Henmore
Brook. If a goal has been scored by 5 p.m. a new ball is turned up
and play starts afresh. Scorers keep the balls so every year new ones
have to be made. The game is played both on Shrove Tuesday and Ash Wednesday.

At one time the ball was turned up in the Market Place and the background
illustration (shown here) from an old painting portrays a Shrovetide Football crowd
in the early 1860s. Every face was a
portrait of an Ashbourne character and
the pub on the left is the *George
and Dragon*.

Royal Shrovetide Football is one of
Derbyshire's many ancient customs which
have survived into the last decades of the
twentieth century and looks set to endure into the
twenty first. It serves a useful purpose in bringing
tourists into the town, in
providing amusement to the
people of the town and
allows young people to
work off their
aggressions and let off
steam in a relatively
harmless way.

*Local celebrity Phil Drabble
launches a game*

ON ASHBOURNE'S DOORSTEP

"Was you ever in Dovedale? I assure you there are things in Derbyshire as noble as in Greece or Switzerland"

Lord Byron

St. Oswald's spire at sunset.

CARSINGTON WATER

About five miles to the east of Ashbourne is the newly created reservoir known as Carsington Water. It has a visitor centre, car parks, restaurants, sailing club, water sports base, footpaths, bridleways and a bicycle hire centre.

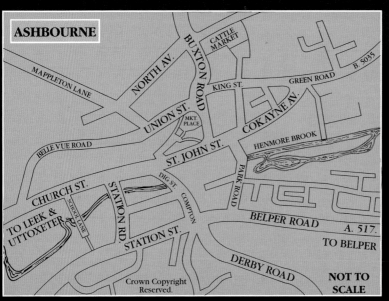

ASHBOURNE

Crown Copyright Reserved.

NOT TO SCALE